GREAT NORTHERN RAILWAY
1945 THROUGH 1970
VOLUME 2
PHOTO ARCHIVE

Iconografix Inc. exists to preserve history through the publication of notable photographic archives and the list of titles under the Iconografix imprint is constantly growing. Transportation enthusiasts should be on the Iconografix mailing list and are invited to write and ask for a catalog, free of charge.

Authors and editors in the field of transportation history are invited to contact the Editorial Department at Iconografix, Inc., PO Box 446, Hudson WI 54016. We require a minimum of 120 photographs per subject. We prefer subjects narrow in focus, e.g., a specific model, railroad, or racing venue. Photographs must be of high-quality, suited to large format reproduction.

GREAT NORTHERN RAILWAY
1945 THROUGH 1970
VOLUME 2
PHOTO ARCHIVE

Edited with introduction by
Byron D. Olsen

Iconografix
Photo Archive Series

Iconografix
PO Box 446
Hudson, Wisconsin 54016 USA

Iconografix books are offered at a discount when sold in quantity for promotional use. Businesses or organizations seeking details should write to the Marketing Department, Iconografix, at the above address.

Library of Congress Card Number: 97-75285

ISBN 1-882256-79-4

98 99 00 01 02 03 04 5 4 3 2 1

Cover and book design by Shawn Glidden

Printed in the United States of America

PREFACE

The histories of machines and mechanical gadgets are contained in the books, journals, correspondence, and personal papers stored in libraries and archives throughout the world. Written in tens of languages, covering thousands of subjects, the stories are recorded in millions of words.

Words are powerful. Yet, the impact of a single image, a photograph or an illustration, often relates more than dozens of pages of text. Fortunately, many of the libraries and archives that house the words also preserve the images.

In the *Photo Archive Series,* Iconografix reproduces photographs and illustrations selected from public and private collections. The images are chosen to tell a story—to capture the character of their subject. Reproduced as found, they are accompanied by the captions made available by the archive.

The Iconografix *Photo Archive Series* is dedicated to young and old alike, the enthusiast, the collector and anyone who, like us, is fascinated by "things" mechanical.

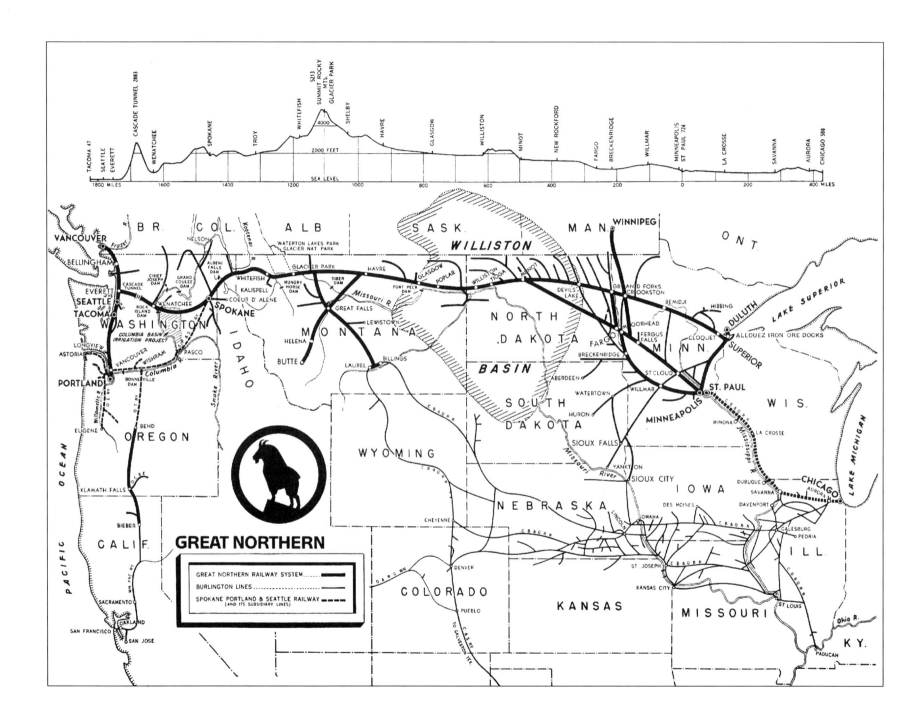

6

INTRODUCTION

This is the second volume of photographs of the Great Northern Railway I have compiled and edited. Like in the first volume, these photographs were taken in the years following World War II until March 1970, when the Great Northern became part of the new Burlington Northern. Like the first volume, some of the photographs in this book are from Great Northern archives or were taken by Hedrich Blessing Studios working for Great Northern. Unlike the first volume, however, the majority of the photos in this photo archive were taken by me in the 1950s and 1960s.

I grew up in St. Paul, Minnesota, and Great Northern had long been my favorite railroad. I counted myself fortunate indeed to be hired by Great Northern in 1967 and work in my chosen profession as a lawyer for the company until the Burlington Northern merger ended the existence of Great Northern forever.

The Great Northern was based in St. Paul and began its existence as the St. Paul & Pacific. Its first revenue passenger service began on June 28, 1862, between St. Paul and the city of St. Anthony, which later became Minneapolis. From that date until it passed out of existence on March 2, 1970, Great Northern was a favorite of railroad enthusiasts and Wall Street investors alike. Always colorful—and nearly always profitable—Great Northern was never in receivership or bankruptcy, unlike most of its competitors at sometime or another.

Thirty years after Great Northern officially disappeared, most of its route system lives on carrying more traffic than ever as the main lines of the Burlington Northern Sante Fe in the northern tier states. Burlington Northern was formed out of a combination of Great Northern Railway; Northern Pacific Railway; Chicago Burlington and Quincy; Spokane, Portland and Seattle; and Pacific Coast Railroad, to name the most important components. Later, Burlington Northern acquired the St. Louis-San Francisco Railroad, better known as the Frisco. On September 22, 1995, Burlington Northern merged with the Atchison, Topeka and Sante Fe to form the Burlington Northern Sante Fe—a huge system. Railroad enthusiasts and rail historians were delighted when the merged company painted one of the first orders of new locomotives a modern version of the Great Northern color scheme of Omaha orange and dark green and even included yellow striping. This paint scheme was a refreshing acknowledgment of one of the illustrious predecessors of the Burlington Northern Sante Fe. The new company also uses paint schemes of other predecessor roads.

Many of the identifications of diesel locomotive types in this book do not mention a manufacturer. Most of the Great Northern diesel electric fleet was built by General Motors Electro Motive Division (EMD). Although Great Northern rostered some Alcos, Baldwins, and other obscure brands, EMD power was favored and other brands were soon sold off. In the mid 1960s, General Electric entered the main line diesel electric locomotive market and over the years has become a serious competitor to EMD. But while Great Northern was still operating independently, only a few General Electric locomotives found their way onto the roster.

In this book, any reference to GP, SD, E, FT, F3 and F7 locomotives are all EMD built. There are several photos of 500 series E units. All were bought for the first post-war Empire Builder in 1945 and 1947, but soon relegated to other trains. The E units with two unpowered axles per locomotive could not handle the long Empire Builder and Western Star trains on mountain grades. But these long, graceful, swift locomotives became the mainstay power of the rest of the Burlington Northern passenger fleet.

I would like to express thanks to my able and faithful typist, Debi Prozinski, as well as several reference sources. The Great Northern Railway Historical Society, of which I am proud to be a member, continues to do an excellent and thorough job of documenting Great Northern history. Great Northern publicity material, corporate records and car and locomotive diagram books were consulted. Two books by enthusiastic champions of the Great Northern, Charles R. Wood and his wife, Dorothy, continue to be invaluable reference sources on many aspects of Great Northern operations. They are *Lines West* and *The Great Northern Railway: A Pictorial Study*, by Charles and Dorothy Wood. Also valuable was the most significant history of the company yet published, *The Great Northern Railway: A History*, written by a group of authors led by Don L. Hofsommer. Finally, William D. Middleton's definitive work on main line electrification in North America, *When the Steam Roads Electrified*, provided data on the Great Northern electrification.

Byron D. Olsen
St. Paul, Minnesota
May, 1998

The eastbound Red River inches across the Stone Arch Bridge on October 2, 1961. E unit 509 is in charge and running the wrong way because the bridge is being repaired.

The Red River approaches the University of Minnesota main campus, Minneapolis, trailed by beautiful round end observation car 1147.

It's late afternoon on an April day in 1962, and this passenger train passes the University of Minnesota campus, heading for the Stone Arch Bridge and downtown Minneapolis.

Four FT diesels bring a freight through the Midway District of St. Paul. In May 1961 these units approach two decades of service, but still look sharp and well maintained.

NW2 switcher No. 104 pauses at Main Street in northeast Minneapolis in the fall of 1960. Although built in 1939, the locomotive is just out of the paint shop and looks brand new.

In a classic scene of Great Northern prairie railroading, a long freight on the Willmar line, west of Benson, Minnesota, rolls by on November 13, 1961.

Three GP20s of the 2000 series head the train—all are just a year old.

Spiffy caboose X34 carries the markers just behind a tri-level rack car carrying brand-new 1962 Ford Fairlanes, in the days before auto carriers were fully enclosed to reduce damage en route.

EMD E unit 510, wearing the simplified color scheme of the mid 1960s, passes Western Avenue in St. Paul.

GP20 No. 2003 rests beside the Dale Street Shops in St. Paul. This locomotive is set up to run long nose forward, as were all GP and SD types on Great Northern until the arrival of the GP30s with full vision cabs. It's June 1964.

Two Baldwins and SD7 No. 564 at the Dale Street Shops in St. Paul. It's March 1962 and the SD is ten years old.

Great Northern's first General Electric diesel locomotive, seen here in 1967, has just been freshly painted in the new Big Sky blue color scheme. It's a U25B.

GP9 No. 707 and an F unit get some attention in this March 1962 view inside the Dale Street Shops, St. Paul.

The engine overhaul bay at the Dale Street Shops, St. Paul, in 1962.

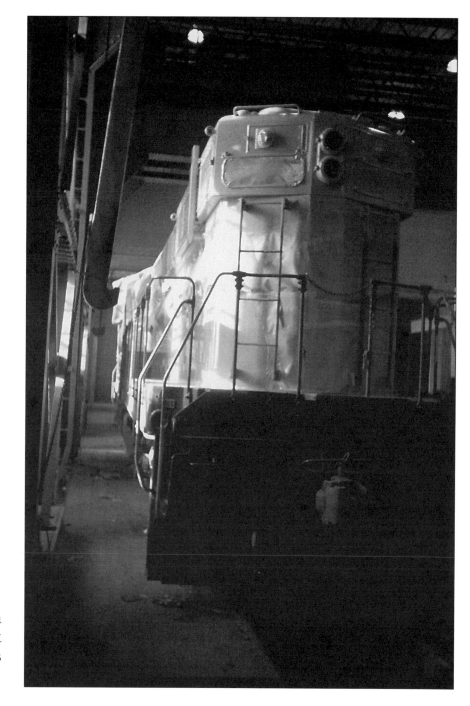

An SD gets repainted at Dale Street, St. Paul, in March 1962. This is one of the last locomotives to get repainted before a simplified color scheme was adopted a year later.

The Red River thunders across the bridge onto Nicollet Island, slowing quickly for the Minneapolis passenger station just minutes away. The year is 1961.

The Red River observation car passes across Nicollet Island. The year is 1961.

It's 8:45 AM on an October day in 1961. The morning Badger pulls out of the Minneapolis Great Northern passenger station and eases around the tight curve, past the depot powerhouse onto the Mississippi River bridge.

E unit 508 about to step onto Nicollet Island. Today the Minneapolis Depot is gone, but the Great Northern line across Nicollet Island still is used heavily. The bridge in this photo has been replaced with a through truss.

A variety of locomotives at the fueling track, Minneapolis Junction, August 1962. GP9 No. 660 occupies center stage, flanked by two FTs, and an F7.

Still looking good after close to three decades of service, a pair of FT A units rest at Minneapolis Junction in 1962.

A handsome pair of F7s trailed by a GP are prepared for a road service assignment in Minneapolis in October 1961. F7A No. 464A was built in 1953.

The face that dieselized America's railroads. A pair of Great Northern F units rest in Minneapolis in 1961 with a Baldwin switcher in the background. FT unit 412A was delivered in 1944.

Caboose line up in northeast Minneapolis, featuring nearly new caboose X46 in 1961.

A passenger train cruises through northeast Minneapolis near University Avenue in 1961. EMD E unit No. 511 is in charge.

The inbound Red River passes through northeast Minneapolis a few minutes from the Minneapolis Depot.

The Minneapolis Great Northern Depot in 1964. The sign on the roof lists all the railroads using the station. The Great Western Warehouse to the left of the depot was originally a Wisconsin Central Freighthouse. By 1997 only the Grain Belt beer sign in the distance survives.

The Western Star prepares to depart the Minneapolis Great Northern Station on April 7, 1962. There is a dome car in the consist today, normally found only on the Empire Builder.

The westbound Western Star pulls out of the Minneapolis Depot, trailing a long string of baggage/mail cars behind the passenger cars. It's April 1962.

It's March 1969 and the Western Star prepares to depart Minneapolis, pulled by a nearly new SDP45 delivered in Big Sky blue. This is Great Northern's first use of road switcher type locomotives to pull main line passenger trains.

A view of the Western Star from the cab in March 1969. The few passenger cars are sandwiched between several mail and express cars on both the head end and rear end of the train. The end of the Great Northern is one year away and Amtrak will take over passenger service in two years.

Fireman's view from the Western Star, heading for Willmar, Minnesota.

Cab interior of an E7 passenger locomotive about to depart St. Paul Union Depot for Duluth with the morning Badger in December 1969.

The morning sun lights the side of a westbound passenger train at 9 AM, October 27, 1966, passing Raymond Avenue in St. Paul.

Engineer's view of the Stone Arch Bridge in downtown Minneapolis from the cab of an E7. That skyline has undergone vast changes since this photo was taken in December 1969.

The southbound Badger, seen from the cab of the northbound, near Cambridge, Minnesota, in 1969.

The northbound Badger heading for Duluth passes near Askov, Minnesota. It's April 5, 1963, and spring has not yet made much of an impression on northern Minnesota.

On the morning of April 5, 1963, the northbound Badger stops for passengers at Kerrick, Minnesota. The morning Badger between Duluth and the Twin Cities was a local, making stops at every small town. The afternoon Gopher was an express, making only one intermediate stop en route at Sandstone.

Unusual visitors crowd the bumper posts at the Duluth Union Station. That's the open platform of a Great Northern business car in the foreground, and the observation car *Little Chief Mountain* No. 1295 is on the far track.

Great Northern business car A10 occupies Track Four in Duluth. This car was originally built as compartment/observation car 766 and converted for business use in 1924. When the photo was taken, the car was almost sixty years old.

It's the mid 1960s and E unit 510 prepares to depart Duluth Union Station for the Twin Cities. Fortunately, the elegant depot has been preserved and today the Lake Superior Railroad Museum occupies these tracks with a fine collection of historic railroad equipment.

Two SD7s spot ore cars on the Allouez docks in Superior, Wisconsin, in late 1969.

At the Allouez ore docks in Superior, Wisconsin, EMD SD No. 557 spots ore cars for unloading into the bins that will transfer the ore into ships. That's Duluth and the North Shore of Lake Superior in the distance.

The ore vessel "Cliff's Victory" rides low in the water as it is filled with iron ore from the Great Northern docks. The waiting steamer at the end of the dock rides higher because it is empty. The chutes in the foreground lower to let ore pour by gravity into the hold of the ships.

Stacking roofs at Great Northern car shops in St. Cloud, Minnesota, where they will be assembled into new boxcars.

Great Northern FT No. 403-D, built in 1945, leads another FT and an F7 B unit pulling a short freight somewhere out in the wide open spaces of western Minnesota or the Dakotas.

A lineup of new Big Sky blue covered hopper cars is loaded with wheat, the life blood of the Great Northern. It's Montana 1968, and covered hoppers are by this time well on the way to replacing boxcars as the preferred car for grain loading.

It is a cold day in 1969 at Northgate, North Dakota, on the Canadian border as a unit train of covered hopper cars is loaded with potash trucked down from Canada for International Mineral and Chemical Corporation.

Great Northern's newly inaugurated potash unit train trundles south from Northgate, North Dakota, in 1969, led by six EMD F units newly painted Big Sky Blue for this service.

New International Harvester farm equipment posed symbolically against a huge grain elevator, which these machines will soon be helping to fill.

An eastbound freight runs along the middle fork of the Flathead River near Glacier National Park, pulled by a matched set of EMD F7 A and B units.

Vermiculite insulation is piped across the Kootenai River and loaded into railcars near Libby, Montana.

Along the main line in Montana, fresh ballast is graded to a precise contour.

Cleaning boxcars in 1959 at Gavin Yard near Minot, North Dakota. After removing loose debris and sweeping, live steam and high pressure hot water prepare boxcars for their next load.

A new bridge over the Skykomish River nears completion in the Cascade Mountains of Washington state. This bridge was part of a major line change near Index, Washington, which permitted a significant shortening of the Great Northern main line.

A pair of brand-new EMD F45 locomotives spliced by another new road unit haul a short freight south along Puget Sound between Everett and Seattle in 1969. Great Northern bought thirteen of these wide-bodied locomotives just before the Burlington Northern merger in March 1970, and ten more arrived shortly thereafter.

King Street Station, Seattle, with the landmark LC Smith Tower in the distance. It's 2:50 PM, March 24, 1970, and the afternoon International for Vancouver, British Columbia, is being readied for a 3 PM departure. The tail car is No. 1293, the *Cathedral Mountain*, one of the beautiful high window mountain series observation cars. It will be a lovely place from which to watch Puget Sound unroll past the windows.

The Seattle section of the Empire Builder prepares to leave King Street Station for St. Paul and Chicago. It is just three weeks after the Burlington Northern merger has ended the official existence of the Great Northern, but there is already a car in Burlington Northern green and white livery in the train.

The fueling track at Interbay Yard, Seattle, in March 1970.

The Empire Builder rolls north along Puget Sound toward Everett where it will turn east for the Midwest and Chicago.

Puget Sound from the back platform of the eastbound Empire Builder.

The Empire Builder pauses briefly in Everett, Washington. Sleeper 1264, the *Bad Axe River*, carries the markers, and the porter has just advised that it's time to get aboard.

The Empire Builder climbs the Cascades in early 1970. Most of the cars have been repainted Big Sky blue, but the Burlington Northern merger requires everything to be repainted again in Cascade green and white.

The Empire Builder passes a westbound freight headed by SD45 No. 410, three years after the locomotive was built. The Builder climbs the Cascades in Washington state.

The beautiful but rugged Cascade Mountains—the most formidable topographic barrier on the entire Great Northern main line.

Y-class Electric locomotive No. 5011 was one of several built for the 1927 electrification of Great Northern lines through the Cascade Mountains in Washington state. The electrified zone extended from Wenatchee to Skykomish, a distance of 71 miles, and included the seven mile long Cascade Tunnel. Brand-new No. 5011 is tested at the General Electric plant in Erie, Pennsylvania, where it was built.

Another view of electric locomotive No. 5011 rebuilt with EMD diesel cabs after being totally destroyed in a derailment during World War II. The scene is Wenatchee, Washington, with a train of heavyweight passenger cars in the late 1940s.

One of two W-class electric locomotives in a siding near Skykomish, Washington. Locomotive 5018 and its sister, 5019, were built in 1946 by General Electric and saw only ten years of service before the Great Northern electrification was dismantled in 1956.

A side view of W-class 5018 shows its immense length. These locomotives were 101 feet long and weighed 360 tons. All twelve axles were powered and generated a total of 5,000 horsepower, making them the most powerful single unit locomotives ever built, as of 1946.

This gas electric car was rebuilt in 1946 and streamlined to serve as the power unit of a baby streamliner used to connect Great Falls, Montana, with mainline passenger service at Havre, Montana. It was unique on the Great Northern roster and was scrapped in 1957.

The Great Northern's only Budd Rail Diesel car (RDC). No. 2350 was built in 1956 and Great Northern ran its wheels off—first in northern Minnesota and then running all over Montana on the secondary lines between Great Falls, Billings, Butte and Havre. The RDC remained in service until Amtrak took over passenger service in 1971.

Gas electric car No. 2332 was built in 1929 by a predecessor of EMD. These self-propelled cars could pull a coach or two and were more economical to operate over light density branch lines than locomotive hauled trains. Great Northern had a fleet of thirty of these as late as 1950, and No. 2332 lasted until 1959.

A string of brand-new bright red Great Northern boxcars near Snelling Avenue in St. Paul. These cars were built in 1964 and are unique in having both a sliding door and a plug door, making them suitable for a wide variety of commodities.

Looking like a page from an EMD catalog, a matched A-B-B-A set of FTs pulls a freight in St. Paul. But it's early 1961 and these units are all at least 15 years old.

An ancient but well-maintained open platform observation car at Dale Street in 1962; it is being used as a test car.

It's an early morning in June 1961 and freshly painted E unit 511 eases the Winnipeg Limited downgrade past the Great Northern Mississippi Street coach yards, heading for the St. Paul Union Depot.

A sunny morning June 5, 1961, at the Great Northern Mississippi Street coach yards in St. Paul. All of the passenger cars and business cars were serviced here; a great dome and business car sit on two of the tracks.

Great Northern business car at Mississippi Street in 1963.

Heavyweight business car A10 at Mississippi Street, St. Paul, carries new Big Sky blue paint and a restyled "Rocky the Goat" drumhead.

Heavyweight business car A8 at Jackson Street in 1969. Although looking up to date with the new Big Sky blue color scheme, this car was actually built by Barney & Smith Car Company in 1908. In the distance is a round end observation car out of service by this time.

Vestibules at Mississippi Street in 1969.

The transfer table pit at Jackson Street in 1969. Despite its up-to-date Big Sky blue paint scheme, business car A12 is actually a much rebuilt, old heavyweight car.

Business car A12 at Mississippi Street, June 5, 1961.

A lineup of varnish at Mississippi Street in April 1962. Several business cars and a Mountain series observation are in the distance.

Business cars and observation cars at Mississippi Street in 1962. The drumhead on the streamline Mountain series observation car says, "Western Star."

Several cars in newly painted Big Sky blue in 1969. The coach to the left carries an experimental paint scheme, which was not adopted, with white around the windows and a gray letter board.

The great dome "River View" and business car A28 rest at Mississippi Street in November 1968. The dome car is partner railroad CB&Q's contribution to the Empire Builder equipment pool; note the CB&Q lettering.

A passenger train climbs the grade past the Mississippi Street coach yards in St. Paul on a June afternoon in 1970.

Steam locomotive No. 2523, a Class P-2 Baldwin 4-8-2 built in 1923, is stored semi-serviceable at Willmar, Minnesota, Engine Terminal in 1961. The rods are removed, but the engine appears still capable of being steamed, long after most other Great Northern steam locomotives have been scrapped.

Diesels and a steam locomotive at the Willmar, Minnesota, Engine Terminal. Steam locomotive No. 2523 was retained for preservation and display near Willmar.

A locomotive lineup at Willmar, Minnesota, in 1961, led by GP7 No. 636.

Two years after the last Great Northern steam locomotive was taken out of service, class 0-8 Mikado, No. 3398 rests in northeast Minneapolis awaiting scrapping.

Switcher 842, an 0-8-0, awaits the torch in 1959.

No. 3224, a class 0-4 Mikado 2-8-2, built by Baldwin in 1920, rests its weary bones after almost forty years of service. Its destination is the scrap yard.

Great Northern class S-2 4-8-4 Northern No. 2584 on display at Havre, Montana. Baldwin built this group of locomotives in 1930 to pull the Empire Builder, and it remains the last steam locomotive to be owned by Great Northern and its successor, Burlington Northern.

NW2 switcher No. 130, built in 1941, switches southeast Minneapolis flour mills on October 2, 1961.

Baldwin switcher No. 26, an S12 built in 1953, pauses in the sun near Raymond Avenue in St. Paul. It's November 1964.

A lineup of late-model road power in June 1967 in Minneapolis. GP35's No. 3031 and 3027, acquired in 1965, lead the lineup.

An F7 B unit No. 307B still in service in 1967. Note how the brand-new SD45 towers over the F7 car body.

Brand-new SD45 No. 406 carrying the simplified orange and black color scheme. Seen here in June 1967, this locomotive had been in service just one year.

General Electric U25B No. 2504—one of the first batch of GE diesels to enter service on the Great Northern—in Minneapolis, 1967.

It is October 1961 in northeast Minneapolis and eleven-year-old GP7 No. 609 still looks fresh.

A batch of brand-new GP30s on November 18, 1963.

Spiffy looking transfer caboose X178 appears as if it had been built with a locomotive frame and trucks. Minneapolis, 1967.

Snowplow X1629 and another plow await the call to duty in November 1961.

Great Northern headquarters and executive offices at 175 East Fourth Street, St. Paul, Minnesota, in 1969, on the eve of the Burlington Northern merger. The entire building became Burlington Northern headquarters on March 2, 1970, when the Burlington Northern came into being. When this photo was taken, buildings across Fourth Street, which had blocked a clear view for years, had been removed. By the 1990s, new buildings once again block this view. This building has the largest floor space of any office building in St. Paul.

Great Northern passenger locomotives rest between runs at the St. Paul Union Depot in May 1968. The F units are used on the Empire Builder and Western Star transcontinental trains, and the E unit will power shorter distance runs.

The Duluth bound Badger passes Snelling Avenue in St. Paul on a March morning in 1963. SD9 No. 592, new in 1958, has already been repainted in the new simplified color scheme.

It's 5:03 PM January 11, 1963, as the Red River pulls into Fargo, North Dakota, with the last vestiges of daylight.

SD7 No. 555 has been freshly repainted and switches cars near Union Yard, Minneapolis, in April 1962.

A work train led by GP7 No. 651 passes near Glencoe, Minnesota, in July 1961.

The Stone Arch Bridge in Minneapolis, one of the Great Northern's foremost engineering landmarks, undergoes repair in 1965. Floodwaters undermined three of the piers, causing the bridge to sag.

One of the first trains over the newly repaired and reopened Stone Arch Bridge, the westbound Western Star. Note the reinforcement under two of the arches.

Another part of the Stone Arch Bridge was disfigured by the insertion of this truss to permit construction of the upper harbor locks on the Mississippi.

In August 1966, the eastbound Empire Builder cruises between Minneapolis and St. Paul past Union Yard, just in from its long trek from Seattle. Early morning mist is still in the air, almost obscuring the great length of the train. The southeast Minneapolis grain elevators in the background are the destination for much of the grain produced on the Great Northern.

The morning sun breaks over Union Yard, Minneapolis, against the backdrop of many grain elevators. By the 1990s, most of Union Yard had been removed, but the main line and most of the grain elevators remained.

A westbound passenger train in charge of E unit No. 505 approaches the Stone Arch Bridge in southeast Minneapolis. It's late afternoon on a March day in 1962 and the train is en route from St. Paul to Minneapolis and points west.

A mixed bag of F units led by F7A 307C, trundles a caboose past Snelling Avenue in St. Paul in 1961. An F3 and two FTs are in the consist.

The Iconografix Photo Archive Series includes:

AMERICAN CULTURE
AMERICAN SERVICE STATIONS 1935-1943	ISBN 1-882256-27-1
COCA-COLA: A HISTORY IN PHOTOGRAPHS 1930-1969	ISBN 1-882256-46-8
COCA-COLA: ITS VEHICLES IN PHOTOGRAPHS 1930-1969	ISBN 1-882256-47-6
PHILLIPS 66 1945-1954	ISBN 1-882256-42-5

AUTOMOTIVE
FERRARI PININFARINA 1952-1996	ISBN 1-882256-65-4
GT40	ISBN 1-882256-64-6
IMPERIAL 1955-1963	ISBN 1-882256-22-0
IMPERIAL 1964-1968	ISBN 1-882256-23-9
LE MANS 1950: THE BRIGGS CUNNINGHAM CAMPAIGN	ISBN 1-882256-21-2
LINCOLN MOTOR CARS 1920-1942	ISBN 1-882256-57-3
LINCOLN MOTOR CARS 1946-1960	ISBN 1-882256-58-1
MG 1945-1964	ISBN 1-882256-52-2
MG 1965-1980	ISBN 1-882256-53-0
PACKARD MOTOR CARS 1935-1942	ISBN 1-882256-44-1
PACKARD MOTOR CARS 1946-1958	ISBN 1-882256-45-X
SEBRING 12-HOUR RACE 1970	ISBN 1-882256-20-4
STUDEBAKER 1933-1942	ISBN 1-882256-24-7
STUDEBAKER 1946-1958	ISBN 1-882256-25-5
VANDERBILT CUP RACE 1936 & 1937	ISBN 1-882256-66-2

TRACTORS AND CONSTRUCTION EQUIPMENT
CASE TRACTORS 1912-1959	ISBN 1-882256-32-8
CATERPILLAR MILITARY TRACTORS VOLUME 1	ISBN 1-882256-16-6
CATERPILLAR MILITARY TRACTORS VOLUME 2	ISBN 1-882256-17-4
CATERPILLAR SIXTY	ISBN 1-882256-05-0
CLETRAC AND OLIVER CRAWLERS	ISBN 1-882256-43-3
ERIE SHOVEL	ISBN 1-882256-69-7
FARMALL CUB	ISBN 1-882256-71-9
FARMALL F–SERIES	ISBN 1-882256-02-6
FARMALL MODEL H	ISBN 1-882256-03-4
FARMALL MODEL M	ISBN 1-882256-15-8
FARMALL REGULAR	ISBN 1-882256-14-X
FARMALL SUPER SERIES	ISBN 1-882256-49-2
FORDSON 1917-1928	ISBN 1-882256-33-6
HART-PARR	ISBN 1-882256-08-5
HOLT TRACTORS	ISBN 1-882256-10-7
INTERNATIONAL TRACTRACTOR	ISBN 1-882256-48-4
INTERNATIONAL TD CRAWLERS 1933-1962	ISBN 1-882256-72-7
JOHN DEERE MODEL A	ISBN 1-882256-12-3
JOHN DEERE MODEL B	ISBN 1-882256-01-8
JOHN DEERE MODEL D	ISBN 1-882256-00-X
JOHN DEERE 30 SERIES	ISBN 1-882256-13-1
MINNEAPOLIS-MOLINE U-SERIES	ISBN 1-882256-07-7
OLIVER TRACTORS	ISBN 1-882256-09-3
RUSSELL GRADERS	ISBN 1-882256-11-5
TWIN CITY TRACTOR	ISBN 1-882256-06-9

RAILWAYS
CHICAGO, ST. PAUL, MINNEAPOLIS & OMAHA RAILWAY 1880-1940	ISBN 1-882256-67-0
CHICAGO&NORTH WESTERN RAILWAY 1975-1995	ISBN 1-882256-76-X
GREAT NORTHERN RAILWAY 1945-1970	ISBN 1-882256-56-5
GREAT NORTHERN RAILWAY 1945-1970 VOLUME 2	ISBN 1-882256-79-4
MILWAUKEE ROAD 1850-1960	ISBN 1-882256-61-1
SOO LINE 1975-1992	ISBN 1-882256-68-9
WISCONSIN CENTRAL LIMITED 1987-1996	ISBN 1-882256-75-1
WISCONSIN CENTRAL RAILWAY 1871-1909	ISBN 1-882256-78-6

TRUCKS
AMERICAN LaFRANCE 700 SERIES 1945-1952	ISBN 1-882256-90-5
BEVERAGE TRUCKS 1910-1975	ISBN 1-882256-60-3
BROCKWAY TRUCKS 1948-1961*	ISBN 1-882256-55-7
DODGE TRUCKS 1929-1947	ISBN 1-882256-36-0
DODGE TRUCKS 1948-1960	ISBN 1-882256-37-9
DODGE POWER WAGONS 1940-1980	ISBN 1-882256-89-1
LOGGING TRUCKS 1915-1970	ISBN 1-882256-59-X
MACK® MODEL AB*	ISBN 1-882256-18-2
MACK AP SUPER-DUTY TRUCKS 1926-1938*	ISBN 1-882256-54-9
MACK MODEL B 1953-1966 VOLUME 1*	ISBN 1-882256-19-0
MACK MODEL B 1953-1966 VOLUME 2*	ISBN 1-882256-34-4
MACK EB-EC-ED-EE-EF-EG-DE 1936-1951*	ISBN 1-882256-29-8
MACK EH-EJ-EM-EQ-ER-ES 1936-1950*	ISBN 1-882256-39-5
MACK FC-FCSW-NW 1936-1947*	ISBN 1-882256-28-X
MACK FG-FH-FJ-FK-FN-FP-FT-FW 1937-1950*	ISBN 1-882256-35-2
MACK LF-LH-LJ-LM-LT 1940-1956 *	ISBN 1-882256-38-7
MACK MODEL B FIRE TRUCKS 1954-1966*	ISBN 1-882256-62-X
MACK MODEL CF FIRE TRUCKS 1967-1981*	ISBN 1-882256-63-8
MACK MODEL L FIRE TRUCKS 1940-1954*	ISBN 1-882256-86-7
STUDEBAKER TRUCKS 1927-1940	ISBN 1-882256-40-9
STUDEBAKER TRUCKS 1941-1964	ISBN 1-882256-41-7
WHITE TRUCKS 1900-1937	ISBN 1-882256-80-8

The Iconografix Photo Gallery Series includes:

CATERPILLAR PHOTO GALLERY	ISBN 1-882256-70-0
MACK TRUCKS PHOTO GALLERY*	ISBN 1-882256-88-3

The Iconografix Photo Album Series includes:

CADILLAC 1948-1964	ISBN 1-882256-83-2
CORVETTE PROTOTYPES & SHOW CARS	ISBN 1-882256-77-8
DODGE PICKUPS 1939-1978	ISBN 1-882256-82-4
FIRE CHIEF CARS 1900-1997	ISBN 1-882256-87-5
LOLA RACE CARS 1962-1990	ISBN 1-882256-73-5
LOTUS RACE CARS 1961-1994	ISBN 1-882256-84-0
McLAREN RACE CARS 1965-1996	ISBN 1-882256-74-3
PORSCHE 356 1948-1965	ISBN 1-882256-85-9

*This product is sold under license from Mack Trucks, Inc. Mack is a registered Trademark of Mack Trucks, Inc. All rights reserved.

All Iconografix books are available from direct mail specialty book dealers and bookstores worldwide, or can be ordered from the publisher. For book trade and distribution information or to add your name to our mailing list contact

Iconografix
PO Box 446/BK
Hudson, Wisconsin, 54016

Telephone: (715) 381-9755
USA (800) 289-3504
Fax: (715) 381-9756

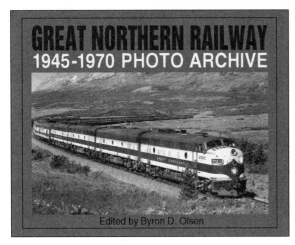
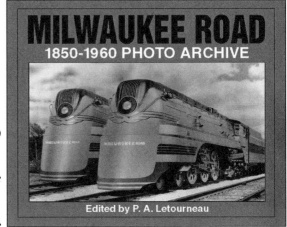

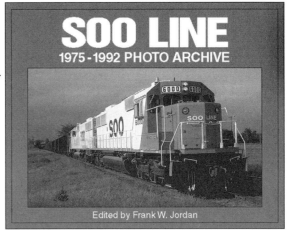
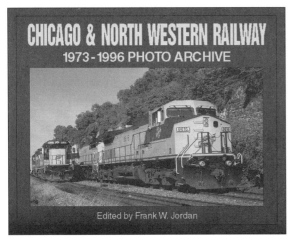